# CHALKDUST

.........................

*thoughts on Salisbury
and its district
at the start of the
new millennium*

First published in 2000
by Salisbury District Council,
Bourne Hill, Salisbury SP1 3UZ

ISBN  0 86080 453 4

Cover photograph: *View to Salisbury from
Near Hole Farm, Clarendon*, by Steve Day, 1999.
Cover map: part of *Wiltonia, sive comitatus
Wiltoniensis*, by Johann Blaeu, 1648, supplied by
Wiltshire County Council, Libraries and Heritage.

CHALKDUST was
edited by John Chandler
designed by Ani Overton Design & Graphics
printed by Salisbury Printing Company Ltd,
Greencroft Street, Salisbury SP1 1JF

# CONTENTS

........................

# *Foreword by Michael Humphreys*

It is a dull grey December afternoon, that no man's land between Christmas and a New Millennium. As the calendar finally turns toward 2000 there is an opportunity to reflect on what has gone before, and anticipate what might be.

One of my interests has been old coins, not as a serious collector, but looking at the way their designs and inscriptions change, commemorating what is happening in the world, or at least what the coin-maker perceives is happening. Each of us perceives our own world in a very personal way. It comes as no surprise when someone relates an event quite differently to the way we ourselves perceived it. These differences have been recognised for many centuries and throughout many cultures. Indeed Pilate asked of the God-Man, whose second millennium we now commemorate, one of the most famous questions of all time "What is Truth?"

The search for Truth has preoccupied men and women throughout the world and over centuries. Columbus sought the truth of the physical world while Michelangelo has left us with his perception of the people around him and latterly Einstein explored and offered an explanation of the universe. Few of us can begin to touch the heights achieved by giants such as Michelangelo or Einstein but each of us has a unique contribution to give to the world.

The new two pound coin is inscribed 'Standing on the Shoulders of Giants'. The achievements of others may offer a stimulus within our own lives and we must not be content to do nothing because some have done so much. The contributions that follow are personal responses in the journey towards Truth. I commend them to you. By searching for our own truths we too can become Giants within our communities and for our children.

MICHAEL HUMPHREYS

## "Milestones need marking if only to set a standard and a point of reference.

*When Councillor Michael Humphreys floated the idea of collecting and collating opinions of life in the area from Salisbury and District young people to form a Millennium work of art, I was all in favour.*

Now Salisbury District Council is publishing this unique and unusual book and making copies available free to students attending all schools in the district.

The editor, designer and printer can all share in Michael's vision, and so can the contributors, **– especially the contributors** – because I know we will all find this an illuminating, stimulating and often amusing little commentary on contemporary life in our city and district which will last for ever and which is bound to touch the lives of the future inhabitants of our tiny corner of the world."

DAVID PARKER
*Chairman,*
*Salisbury District Council*

# 'How do you feel' we asked, '. . .

. . . *about living in South Wiltshire at the end of the twentieth century?*
. . . *about the view from your window?*
. . . *about what you do day by day?*
. . . *about other members of your community?'*

Salisbury Cathedral
**Ryan Libbey**

And you told us. You sent us poems, stories, letters, pictures, comments – hundreds of them. We read them all, and enjoyed your views on living here, and life in general. Now all the entries are to be preserved for the future, as a little capsule of our world. One day historians will explore 'The Chalkdust Archive', as we are calling it, to find out about us.

Meanwhile we have produced this book. Here are the best, most interesting, most revealing, most original of the entries (as we judged them) for us all to enjoy. Alongside everything else produced to celebrate the millennium here is a special souvenir, about us, ordinary people – no, **special** people – living here, now.

The entries come from Salisbury, and from Salisbury District, a beautiful country of river valleys, villages, farms and downland, which surrounds the world-famous cathedral city in South Wiltshire. The landscape is built on chalk and, like footprints in the dust, it bears the imprint of those from previous millennia who have lived and died here. *Chalkdust* is a contribution from us.

My thanks to Salisbury District Council, whose project this is; to Michael Humphreys, who first suggested it; and to Helen Hale, Kate Westgarth and Carolyn Johannesen, who have administered it. Special thanks to Ani Overton, who has designed this book, and to Steven Tilley and his staff, who printed it. And, most important of all, thanks to everyone who contributed an entry, whether or not we could include it here.

JOHN CHANDLER

# CONTRIBUTORS

*Contributors under 16 years old are distinguished by their age (at time of composition) following their names. A few contributors did not include their surnames on their submissions, and their forenames are printed at the end of this list.*

Amy Albery *(15)*

Samantha Albery *(13)*

Katie Allen *(15)*

Rebecca Allender *(10)*

Tim Bacon *(10)*

David Barnett *(14)*

Cloé Bartlett *(9)*

Zoe Berry *(8)*

Julia Blomquist *(7)*

Victoria Bowman *(10)*

Laura Boyd *(7)*

Matthew Budgell *(9)*

Rebecca Bullen *(14)*

Shauni Burt *(8)*

Lauren May Campbell *(8)*

Ellie Carlisle *(14)*

Kerri Chalk *(14)*

Zarah Chappell-King *(13)*

Marie Chevant *(12)*

Emma Cole *(8)*

Amanda Cooper *(13)*

Jenna Copp *(13)*

Lee Cox *(13)*

William Creech *(8)*

Henry Curr *(9)*

James Davies *(9)*

Mrs A. Dean

Lizzie Dixon *(14)*

Peter Douglas *(9)*

Daisy Drury *(14)*

Stuart Dubber *(15)*

Charley Lagler Duff *(7)*

Joanna Newton Dunn *(14)*

Lizzie Edwards *(15)*

Simon Edwards *(8)*

Florence Ellis *(8)*

Michelle Fields *(8)*

Hannah Fisher *(15)*

Miranda Flood *(13)*

Amy Fortis *(9)*

Sophie Freemantle *(8)*

Joel Friskney-Adams *(9)*

Jessica Fulford *(8)*

Miranda Garrett *(14)*

Corinne Gatehouse *(14)*

Peter Gillott

Milly Girling *(6)*

Thomas Glyde *(13)*

Katherine Goddard *(14)*

Tracy Gooding *(14)*

Abigail Goodman *(10)*

Rebecca Gorringe *(9)*

Laura Goss *(13)*

James Beeson Gould *(14)*

Danielle Gray *(9)*

Natasha Griffiths *(11)*

Stephanie Grummitt *(10)*

Robynne Hammer *(15)*

Louis Harbison *(14)*

Zoe Hardiman *(9)*

Hayley Harding *(8)*

Faye Hatton *(13)*

Sarah Hatton *(8)*

Sophie Hayes *(14)*

Ellen Heathcote *(9)*

Katie Helden *(13)*

Philippa Hemsley *(14)*

Lucy Hill *(8)*

Heidi Hitchens *(14)*

Tim Hodson *(13)*

Tracy Hogan *(8)*

Alison Hogg *(13)*

Adrienne Howell

Rose Hughes

William Ibbotson *(11)*

Belinda Jacob *(12)*

Laura Jones *(13)*

Martyn Jones *(14)*

Sarah Kirkpatrick *(9)*

Marc Kusicka *(9)*

Philippa Lawrence *(9)*

Elizabeth Lawson *(7)*

Emma Leighfield *(8)*

Ryan Libbey *(8)*

David Livesey (8)

Ryan Loader (8)

Natasha Long (9)

Emily Ludlow (9)

Katie Luxton (11)

Rebecca Mallichan (9)

Clare Manser (12)

Nicky Marchant (13)

Imogen Marcus (14)

Joe Marks (8)

William Marks (13)

Sarah Mausley

Catherine Mawdsley (14)

Anthony Munro (14)

Chris Mustow (13)

Grace Naug (12)

Miss B.M. Naylor

Lindsay Newell

Matthew Newman (8)

James Ockenden (14)

Timothy Oliver (9)

Mr M.C. Patience

Luke Peckham (8)

Ashley Pennell (8)

Amanda Perry (13)

Lloyd Perry (14)

Luke Pickard (9)

Lucy Phipps (9)

Helen Picknett (12)

Catherine Pink (12)

Craig Podger (14)

Hannah Keegan Podger (8)

Daisy Prangnell (14)

Hannah Purkiss (8)

Edward Purvis (9)

Melanie Rainsley (12)

Rachel Rainsley (13)

Joanna Raisbeck (8)

Lucy Rayward (13)

Alana Richards (7)

Melanie Rigg (12)

Hannah Robinson (13)

Peter Robinson (9)

Lewis Rudman (7)

Sophia Sample (8)

Annie Samuels (13)

Joyce Sanders

Jonathan Scammell (8)

Ella Scott (12)

Alice Scott-Jupp (9)

Hannah Sims (8)

Gemma Skelton (15)

Luke Southwell (8)

Michael Sparrow (13)

Isabel Spring (9)

Samantha Stephen (10)

Emily Taylor (8)

Mrs C.A. Thompson

Richard Thompson (9)

Grace Travis (9)

Nicola Twallin (13)

James Vaughan (8)

Kate Vickery (8)

Kate Walker (13)

Alex Watterston (9)

Arthur Webb (8)

Kristi-Lee White (8)

Aneira Williams (13)

Emilia Williams (13)

Simon Williams (9)

Paul Willock (8)

Sam Wilson (13)

Thomas Woodhouse (9)

David

Isabel

Katie

# AFTER ALL
# THIS IS
# SALISBURY

.........................

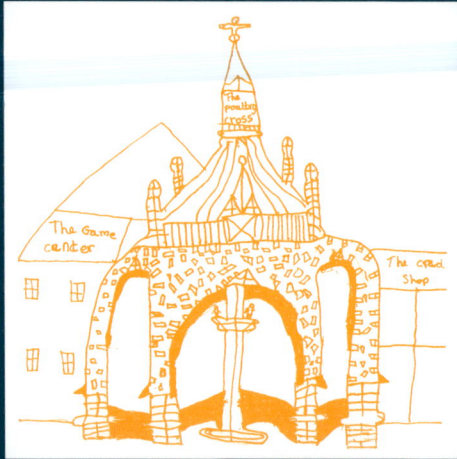

Poultry Cross Matthew Budgell

## MY HOME

I woke up in the morning,
The light shining through my curtains.
I sat up,
I woke up.
It was just a dream.

I looked through my window,
Yet another dark, wet day.
Salisbury.
A typical wet winter morning,
But there still seemed to be happiness.

The Poultry Cross,
The library steps,
The City Hall,
The huge cathedral -
All the things that make Salisbury, Salisbury.

Wet tourists,
A mother with a crying baby,
A young couple with wet chips they can't possibly eat,
Me, cold, sitting in the rain.
Then magic comes -

The rain stops,
The baby calms,
The chips dry,
A happy winter day.
After all this is Salisbury my home.

*Natasha Griffiths*

*After all, this is Salisbury . . .*
*Do we enjoy it, do we appreciate it?*

**WHEN I MOVED TO SALISBURY** in September 1967 I thought l was in heaven. My husband had a change of job and we moved here from Warrington with our three young children.

In those days the change was immense. I had lived for twenty-one years in Manchester and then six years in Warrington. I couldn't believe how lucky I was to be in such a beautiful city, with gardens, parks and rivers which were so clean we could actually see the riverbeds. It was quite astonishing.

There was another surprise – the pace of life was much slower and seemed less materialistic.

I could actually walk half a mile and be in the countryside – It was all unbelievable.

Before moving I'd been warned that Southerners were not friendly and welcoming like 'Folk in the North'. How wrong – our first day here, we had people calling with helpful information about milk deliveries, doctors, schools, dustbin day etc., not to mention the tasty mince pies and tea, and so it went on and before long we had settled in and in no time at all we had a circle of friends.

Thank you Salisbury. We count ourselves fortunate and privileged to have been able to raise and nurture our children in such a 'Green and Pleasant City'.

*A. Dean*

## TO PENPAL

It's me, Rebecca, how are you? I'm fine. So, how's School? Mine's OK. We do English, Science, projects – which is where we do one thing like Tudors for a term or something like that. We also do Maths, RE, Art, Music. That's about all really. Do you do any of those? Well Salisbury is a nice place and has loads of nice things. There's a really good chippy as well. They've got a good library and some nice bookshops. Do you like all your shops? I don't! Do you have a hobby? I do, mine's swimming. I do my swimming at Salisbury Swimming Pool.
I go Monday and Sunday evenings, and Saturday and Thursday mornings. Well if you were looking for a play centre if you came here you could go to Wilton House. That's really cool, because as well as a bit for playing there's a restaurant too! The cinema is really good too! At the moment there's A Bug's Life, the rugrats, ants and Mighty Joe.

I hope you enjoyed the letter - from Rebecca.  1999, April 14th.

*Rebecca Mallichan*

## SALISBURY

Salisbury, Salisbury, buses, cars
Going round and round, up and down.
Lots of places we can go – Wilton House,
Cathedral, Old Sarum.
Some are big, some are small,
Some are fun, and some are boring.
It's a good place to live –
A good place to live.

*William Creech*

Cathedral *Zoe Berry*

OH, I SAID

Oh! Salisbury is great.
Salisbury –
Oh, I said,
Salisbury is a great place to live.
There are lots of places to go
(echo)
There are lots of places to go.
Stonehenge!
Cathedral!
Swimming Pool!
Oh! Salisbury is great!

Salisbury –
Oh, I said,
Salisbury is a great place to live.
There are lots of things to do.
Cycling!
Seeing Sights!
Go to the Library!
Victoria Park and
Cinema!
OH! SALISBURY
IS GREAT!

*Emily Taylor*

Stonehenge *Thomas Woodhouse*

Salisbury City Supporter *Ryan Loader*

## SALISBURY IS MY BIRTHPLACE.

Salisbury is my birthplace.
Salisbury is my home.
I never want to leave it.
I never want to roam.

Many things are ancient.
Many things are new.
There's lots and lots of places.
And always things to do.

The countryside is peaceful.
The countryside is fine.
I like to walk around it,
And make believe it's mine.

Salisbury has five rivers
That come together here.
They make the city what it is,
As history shows us clear.

From most of last millennium
To next one bright and new.
The city keeps its character
The same as me and you.

*Helen Picknett*

HELLO, I AM MARIE, a French girl. I am living in Salisbury because my father is in the army. I have been in lots of other countries like in Germany or United States. I have left France when I was only six years old. Now I am living here, in England, where I will spend two more years and, may be, after I will go back in my country. But right now, I am here, so let's talk about this town, Salisbury.

Salisbury was not as I figure it out. I thought it would be like the others towns where I used to live. At first, I did not really want to go over here, but I had to. So here we go for another country, again. This is not really great to leave your friends to go somewhere you don't even know.

What a surprise when you arrive and see this town so wonderful (even if driving on the other side of the road is not easy)! All this monuments to visit are so great! The Cathedral is so high and so beautiful! This temple, Stonehenge, is so old! How could it stand up on its stones! And all the others things to see.

Well, after this first day in Salisbury, I was sad about what I said of this town, who is may be the prettiest town I had ever seen!

I really like Salisbury!

*Marie Chevant*

A FEW DAYS AGO I realised that the place I live in, Salisbury, is really historic and fun.

I had a brill tour of the cathedral, seeing all the lovely stained glass windows, tombs of knights and ladies, the old clock and the Magna Carta. The Close has some famous residents – Sir Edward Heath, the former Conservative prime minister, and Leslie Thomas the author.

Salisbury Museum is also in the Close and tells the history of Salisbury. I enjoyed reading the signs and looking at the pictures. It has also got other things like old toys.

I like Old Sarum. It's amazing that it used to be a castle where people lived and fought battles.

Salisbury College is good, too. It has different classes and some students do plays.

There is a really good variety of shops for all ages. Some of the shops are housed in old Tudor buildings, like Debenhams. The Haunch of Venison public house is one of the oldest buildings in Salisbury.

I have found that Salisbury is excellent, and I can now safely say that Salisbury is brilliant.

*Abigail Goodman*

HI! IT'S ME

I am writing to you today to tell you about my everyday life, so let's start. Well, first the facts. I live in a place called Salisbury. It's a very small town with lots of friendly people in it.

I find when I go to town, I see quite a lot of tourists along my way, but I mostly see them at the cathedral. There's quite a lot of people there. Oh, in case you don't know, Salisbury is very famous for its cathedral.

Just outside Salisbury there's a place called Stonehenge, and that's known to be very famous as well. And the good part about tourists coming to see Stonehenge is that they always come in to Salisbury.

Now moving on into town there's a lot of shops here like music shops and kind of stuff like that. Now if you're a girl you're bound to like Claire's Accessories – it's packed full of hair accessories and fluffy purses. It's really nice. Oh, there's Smith's which is packed full of pencils, pens, videos and CDs. Everyone likes Smith's. Then there's Woolworth's, with a cafe, crockery, and here comes the best part – Woolworth's has lots of SWEETS! in the centre of the shop, yum yum. Then in the market square we have an ice-cream van which sells all kinds of flavours. They taste gorgeous. I can taste them right now.

Where I live is a place called Bishopdown, and it's got lots of parks to play in, and I've got lots of my friends there. I forgot to tell you, Bishopdown is really big, and it isn't really a place – it's an estate, a massive estate. I love living in Bishopdown.

*Isabel*

## So, Salisbury has plenty of enthusiasts. But there are a few criticisms too . . .

I HAVE LIVED IN SALISBURY for around five years. I used to live in London, and for me and my family it was a great change to start living in a peaceful environment.

Salisbury for my mother wasn't the ideal place to live, as she was used to more shopping centres, more noise and more action. But still, she loved to go and see tourist places like the Cathedral or Stonehenge, even though, after the tenth time it becomes a bit uninteresting (well for me, anyway). For my Dad it was totally different. He used to say, 'I have always wished to live somewhere where I can smell and breathe the clean air.' and would start up again on the same lecture about how me and my brother were really lucky to live in such a healthy environment at such a young age.

Well, I suppose I agree in some ways... The advantage of living in Salisbury is that if I still lived in London, I don't think my mother would let me go to town on my own, but as Salisbury is so safe, my mother is pleased to let me go to town on my own. But then again, going to town is about the only thing to do in Salisbury for my age, and in my eyes teenagers have nothing better to do so start drinking or taking drugs. So I think Salisbury should build an ice-skating rink or a bowling alley, so that there's something else to do besides going to town.

Apart from that I could never dream of living somewhere else as Salisbury is the most perfect little town for me!

*Catherine Pink*

Poultry Cross *Emily Alice Ludlow*

I HAVE LIVED IN SALISBURY for all my life and my opinions have altered with my age. As I go through school, I learn more about the history and the culture. I find it interesting learning about this but to a certain extent I feel it is always being thrown in our faces.

I am appreciative of the Cathedral and other such grand buildings. They bring much tourism to Salisbury and are recognised all over the south of England. However at my age, my idea of fun is not a trip round the Cathedral!!

Salisbury and its general attitude cater for the older inhabitants. The night life is not up to much. The few night clubs it has have a high age limit and are expensive to gain access to. I have done much research on this fact! The public houses are popular but this has its age limit again. This just is encouraging the young people to drink as there is no other activity.

Salisbury is a very friendly city and hopefully it will always remain one. For such a small city it has a lot of interesting history. The shopping mall has a wide range of goods, although small shops. There are many restaurants and fast food places which are popular with young and old people.

*Katie Helden*

# THINGS TO SEE, BOTH COMMON AND RARE

........................

Kite flying, Laverstock *Luke Southwell*

***More criticisms later. Meanwhile
let's explore some of the highlights
of town and countryside.***

AS SHE TRUDGED ALONG TO SCHOOL
It was always Becky's rule
To keep her head up in the sky
And watch the Cathedral as she passed by.

Alas, one morning, her eyes astray,
Hopped on a bus that came her way,
Not realising where she'd gone or come,
Until that journey by bus was done.

As she stood there in dismay,
It dawned on her, she was far away,
Just in front of where she stood
Was a henge of stone, not a wood.

It was a splendid sight to behold,
All through the wind, the rain, the cold,
It's stood there for visitors to roam
And to Becky's delight only ten miles from home.

She left Stonehenge and found a river,
With her head still as high as ever.
Watching the birds dip and fly around,
The sun appeared to sink into the ground.

A long trek home, but she didn't care.
There were things to see, both common and rare.
The fox, the geese, a heron or stork,
Really quite a pleasant walk.

She passed Old Sarum on her right.
A popular place to fly a kite.
It's said from here an arrow went astray,
And as a result, a new place to pray.

Past Poultry Cross, where chickens were sold,
On to the theatre where stories are told.
Florence once worked in the hospital, near,
And down in the cellars they used to brew beer.

Over Long's Bridge, where Constable drew,
And Moonrakers cheated the king's revenue.
Pass by the mill, on the old River Nadder,
Don't worry, the ghost of the leper won't grab-ya.

Now since then our Becky is travelled,
Mysteries of north and south unravelled.
She has even been from east to west,
But always come home 'coz Salisbury is best.

*Rebecca Bullen*

*Tanks on Salisbury Plain Luke Peckham*

## THE WONDERS OF SALISBURY PLAIN

Salisbury Plain is a wide area of grassy fields and woods that winding rivers manage to majestically flow through. Although peaceful this can often be interrupted by the large army camps that populate the area with small green army barracks.

On clear days, I can hear the loud bangs and crashes of the big guns and tanks, from where I live on the other side of Salisbury, and you can tell when the guns are being fired, because there are big red warning flags lining the edge of the practice areas telling you there are exercises going on to try and stop you going in and getting hurt, because they use proper live explosives to train. The exercises can range from basic army manoeuvres to fully armoured tank battles that are marked with luminous tank crossing signs.

However it is not all army camps and fighting exercises, because as you drive along the pleasant winding roads, you can come across a peaceful country village that has been untouched by the routines of the army. Along with this comes

Stonehenge, a wonderful circle of tall stone pillars that attract tourists from every corner of the world. But the mystery is still there about how the stone was got from out of the sea and brought all the way up to the plain.

Farmers also use the open space for grazing their cattle on or growing crops, and you tend to find the desolate farm villages when you get lost on one of the small windy roads that seem to go on for ever, until you come across a major road cutting straight through the landscape like a gash in a person's arm. One of these desolate villages is the village of Imber, which the army asked the people to leave in World War Two, and have never let them back in again. The church and all the houses and shops are still there untouched but there are no people.

As you can see there are lots of original and untouched things about it and I find it very interesting.

*Sam Wilson*

Me *Kate Vickery*

I have blue eyes.
I hate big flies.
I have brown hair.
It's not very fair.
I'm tall and thin,
Just bone and skin.
Percy is my fear,
Whom I won't go near.
I go to Avondale School.
I swim in the pool.
I also have a witch's cat.
And that's the end of that...

Bonna *Sarah Mausley*

... I live in a farm house. We have five bedrooms and a big kitchen. I have two brothers, who are ten and twelve. I am eight years old.

I have lovely toys. I love Sindy my doll. I have a plastic kitchen with pretend food. I love to dress up in dresses. But what I love most of all is my china dolls. I have five of them – they are very pretty. Outside I have a trampoline. It is fourteen feet wide. I can do flips and kicks on it.

On the farm I have three ponies, six hens, a cockerel called Percy. He attacks me. I am frightened of him. The ponies names are Jet, Findlay and Pushkin. Pushkin is the smallest and he is the one I learnt to ride on.

*Kate Vickery*

I'VE RECENTLY MOVED
FROM NEAR LONDON, so my
views on Salisbury are new. I'm
sitting at my kitchen table
looking out at the beautiful
countryside. There's a lady
going by, who's just come out
of her little cherry tree cottage.
She gives a welcoming smile,
and then passes on. That's the
best thing I like about Salisbury.
The friendliness and the
relaxed attitude to everything.
Also I love the smells, the
blossom, the freshly cut grass,
and not forgetting the
muck-spreading smell!

*Lucy Rayward, Fovant*

Valley around my house

Is beautiful, though no

Eagles, but lots of buzzards above

Where rabbits play.


Fabulous countryside, though

Rats all around.

On the hillside, our

Mad horses frolic.


Mice are a'plenty,

Young mice nest in the straw, but


Why so cold

In winter? So

Nice, but

Damp and draughty

Outside, but absolutely

Wonderful!

*Stephanie Grummitt*

My Garden *Simon Edwards*

Old Sarum *Lewis Rudman*

Living in Wiltshire
Is so peaceful.
Flowers bloom everywhere
Even in the smallest places.

In the garden birds are
Nesting in the trees.

Kestrel *Tim Bacon*

Welcoming people to greet you,
Interesting buildings to see.
Local people are so friendly –
Talk to each other,
Smiling on the street.
Hopefully things won't change.
In a way,
Really I like living here,
Even on a winter's day.

*Victoria Bowman*

Stonehenge *Peter Robinson*

## STONEHENGE

Stonehenge *Rebecca Mallichan*

If the Stones had voices what
forgotten tales would they tell?
Of their creators, Stone Age
Warriors from above or below
uniting together to form a
friendship glow.

They are healers by the Sun
contrasting a light so strong in
hope to end confusion and pain.

They make an energy of power
and sorcery leading magic into
the minds of glory.

Merlin's hidden Diamond cave
sparkling history of King Arthur
and his Knights of the round
table. Beautiful Guinevere such
a Queen to save and Lancelot, a
faithful and brave guard.

The Summer Solstice a time of
celebration, dancers from the
Pagans and Druids.
Worshipping Mother Earth
their creator.

The dancers joyfully singing,
having fun.
There is also a history of excitement.

Crop circles, they know how
they appear.
True or false, do we have
to fear?
Do they come by aliens or
wanderers wild?
Who knows the magic of now?

From sunrise to sunset, what a
full life to live.
They would tell us how to be
and live in harmony.

To me, Stonehenge is a place of
peace and magic.
Full of energy and power.
Stonehenge is a place of beauty.

*Aneira Williams*

# LOOK *UP* AND
# YOU WILL SEE IT

.........................

*Along with Stonehenge, it hardly needs saying, we are proudest of our Cathedral.*

A TOURIST IN SALISBURY

'Can you tell me please, where is Cathedral?'
A worried looking tourist said.
'Everyone else has found it
But I alone just can't.
I have found your MacDonalds
I have seen your High Street shops.
"Meet later in cathedral",
It says in our brief guide.
But nowhere were there directions!
So what on earth can I do now?
I suppose I can ask *one* more person –
That man with the glasses looks local.
I'll try just *one* more time.'
A bald man with an overcoat
Reading his daily news smiled at me as he waited:
'Why, look UP and you will see it
Looking down on all of us.
The spire the tallest in England
Will always be there for you to find
Just look up in the sky to see it any time.'
Finally I found it
With a few more stops on the way.
Its beauty had me captured.
I no longer cared how long it had taken.
Here I am in the quiet place like heaven.
Here at last is Cathedral
With its head up in the sky.

*Clare Manser*

Cathedral *Marc Kusicka*

Cathedral *Amy Fortis*

I WANTED TO GO TO THE EASTER DAWN SERVICE at Salisbury Cathedral to hear a friend's granddaughter sing. I'd never been to an early service, but afraid of being late, I cycled quickly into the Close and approached the Cathedral from the side, believing this to be the usual 'service' entrance. I passed no-one, and there were no clergy to issue a greeting at the door, nor even a sign to announce the service.

It was dark inside: when I say dark, I mean really dark, with only the glow from the spotlights outside showing through the high windows, and a pale candle light gleaming from somewhere past the nave. I wasn't at all discouraged by this; it could be a 'darkness to light' service and if I moved quietly along, somewhere I'd find several hundred people crouched silently in the dark waiting for something to happen. As well, I remembered a time when I'd walked through a semi-dark cathedral only to find at the furthermost end a hundred people in a quiet chapel service.

I slid one foot along in front of me as I couldn't see the floor at all and needed to allow for the possibility of steps or ramps. Here's where one is thankful for the lack of a crypt or too many uneven gravestones paving the floor, and for a lack of belief in ghosts.

The light of the single candle finally quit appearing to recede in the distance and allowed me to pinpoint it at the back of the chancel. But there was no one tending the single light. I crept further along the side aisle but it was completely black. There could be no-one back there so I stopped to listen in the gloom.

It was almost difficult to keep one's balance in such dark, with no visual reference. But somewhere far away, a voice began to drone in a monotone that could only emanate from a member of the clergy. But where was it coming from? In a cathedral, the sound seems to come from all sides at once. Suddenly added to it was a commotion at the front central door, the one I'd never known to be open before. Someone was complaining about the steps in the dark. Were they lost as well? Should I make myself known at this point?

It was embarrassing to be lost in a place I thought I knew, in a cathedral that had grown bigger overnight, and more ominous. I inched my way back, passing shadowy recumbent knights, to the side door.

The wooden exit chamber felt like a rescue helicopter in a sea of confusion. I clung to the firm metal door handle and listened carefully again before moving back out to the humid, pre-dawn air spotlit like a stage.

I decided quickly what performance I would give and marched confidently up to the large crowd of people now gathered at the North Face around a newly lit bonfire. As though I'd just arrived.

*Joyce Sanders*

Salisbury Cathedral is a magnificent sight,

But it looks even better at night.

That's when it looks just right.

Then you should celebrate with a Turkish Delight.

Salisbury Cathedral is very old,

And inside it's very cold.

All the houses around are sold.

*Peter Douglas*

*For several contributors the Cathedral was bound up with school,
either a school visit, or a service, or just the ever-present view of it
while stuck in the daily schoolbound traffic jam.*

DAY BY DAY

The sweeping of leaves
While he rolls up his sleeves
Starting a day's work in
    the clouds
Children entering the Close to
    go to school
As still sits the cathedral
    standing very tall
While the rain begins to shower
Just lightly sprinkling the trees
    which surrounds
The elegant statue of grey.

Still he sweeps on, picking up
    every single leaf that falls
Till there are none in sight.
The fields are suddenly
    surrounded with children
Playing their everyday sport
Until the teacher calls, 'Over to
    the tennis courts',
And the fields are at rest
    once more.

The organ plays aloud,
Greeting everyone to their seats
As the cold walls begin to echo
The vicar comes and says
    his prayer
And then the cathedral is empty
    once more.

*Kate Walker*

IN THE YEAR OF 1995 my school (Redlynch Primary School) went on an outing to Salisbury Cathedral. We looked around for a while (getting bored), but were then told that we were going up the spire (this sent a light murmur of happiness and hope that we might just be saved from the deadly jaws of total boredom).

So off we went. We were taken through a small door to the left of the main part of the Cathedral, and were led up a very steep spiral staircase. This was the first thing that sent a shiver down my spine, as we all (about thirty of us) had to stick to the wall as we got higher and higher, because there was a thin stone pillar running down the centre with a gap (large enough for me to fall down) around the pillar. As we got about nine metres up I was feeling very insecure because we had been told all the way that we were 'nearly there', but we still weren't there!

Finally. We got there and we were told to look through a small chicken-wire window. To my horror we were (what seemed like) miles from the ground. We then had to walk along some very narrow planks that were getting old, rotten and rather bouncy! The planks were above huge drops and there was only a very wobbly banister to hold on to.

We then got to the clock that made the end of our little trip up the spire.

We were then told we had to face the joys of going all the way back down those stairs (you can imagine the expression on my face!).

*Laura Jones*

I SAT STARING OUT OF THE WINDOW but not actually looking at the view. I had seen it so often it seemed pointless to look again, however exquisite it was. There's the cathedral rising majestically above the city, which was bustling with traffic, the lush green water meadows below us dotted with the odd cow standing by the gleaming blue waters of the River Avon. But I took it for granted.

Being late was inevitable. There are always traffic jams on the Southampton Road. I mentally shook myself and looked properly out of the window, gazing at the cathedral, a monolith dominating the horizon. 'You know, I went up there when they had all that dismal scaffolding up,' I announced to anybody listening. I fell silent; everybody was locked up in their own thoughts.

*Hannah Robinson*

*Cathedral Alison Hogg*

'REMEMBER, GIRLS – CATHEDRAL ON SUNDAY,' announces Mrs Wasley, 'remember to get your boards, cloaks and blazers ready. I want everyone organised on Sunday!'

We all groan. Cathedral is **so** boring, the service is long AND we have to walk down there.

It is now Sunday morning. There is a mad rush - people eating a quick breakfast so they are ready to put on their blazers, cloaks and boards ready to walk down to the Cathedral. I am upstairs in my dorm, brushing my teeth. Ring-ring-ding-a-ling goes the bell, which means we have to go downstairs. I'm late. The next thing I hear is Mrs Laptain: 'Everybody downstairs - NOW!' I run down the wooden stairs and into the cloakroom. I heave on my blazer and then my cloak, then I grab my board off the shelf. I'm ready. We are all arranged into year groups and I link up with my best friend Jenny. We have to walk down in pairs within our year group. Mrs Wasley inspects us all telling us to do up our top buttons, etc... We set off out of the house, down the school drive and out of school and into Salisbury.

When we all reach the bottom of the hill we sigh. We get strange looks from all the shoppers and general people who are in Salisbury for various reasons. We are so embarrassed in our cloaks. But we walk on, trying to hide behind our boards. As we walk, we talk amongst ourselves giggling about how silly we look. When we come to the Cathedral Close we are told to be silent and walk in single file. All we hear now is the house mistresses' occasional 'Ssshhh' and 'Tut-tut'. Suddenly we arrive at the Cathedral: it's big and spectacular - in fact, it's HUGE. We enter the building and sit down... the blu-tac comes out (we always play with it when we're bored!)

*Nicola Twallin*

# INTO THE
# DREADED
# SCHOOL WE GO

........................

*The journey to school, and then school itself. Actually, a few brave souls admitted that they rather enjoy it.*

HERE WE ARE STUCK AGAIN: will I ever get to school? We are stuck where we always are, behind the blue 'Polo' with the pink box of Sainsbury's tissues on the back shelf. The quaint little church on our left, with its small garden filled with colour, and the old stone wall around it reminds us of each day I go to school. There also goes the same middle-aged woman with her briefcase, and smartly dressed walking to the school on our right. She is closely followed by two teenage girls, one riding an up-to-date bicycle, the other walking along beside her, in her school uniform, which is a maroon-coloured jumper with a tartan skirt.

We move forward a bit, and now we are opposite the street sign, which is good, because it means that we should be out on to the busy roundabout, with all the people rushing around, as if the world were going to end any minute. As we get closer to the roundabout, I hear the chugging engines, and the excited noise of children fade into the background and become very distant. There are still many people walking like mad chickens around us and there is that teenage boy standing on the corner, waiting for someone, so he can walk down to their school, which should take quite a bit of time. He is listening to his Walkman again, just watching the world go by, shutting all the busy sounds out.

Now we are next to the church notice board, where it has a picture of a baby, and on a striking yellow sheet, in bold writing are the words"Charity Fête in aid of N.S.P.C.C.'. I wonder how many people actually go to those things. Oh well, here we go, we're off.

*Joanna Newton Dunn*

School Bus *A Richards*

THE BUS IS FILLED WITH SCHOOLGIRLS; their fierce, energetic chatter is exhausting just to listen to.

*Imogen Marcus*

EVERY MORNING as the driver concentrated harder, you could see his tongue begin to poke out the side of his mouth. The consistent chatter behind him seemed not to bother him. The Prep School behind him were busily playing cards like there was no tomorrow. The Fifth and Sixth Forms were sitting with worried looks on their faces as the time for exams drew near, and they thought of the latest piece of course work that was supposed to be handed in last week and was still not started.

*Lizzie Dixon*

ONLY TEN MINUTES INTO THE LESSON and I was already switched off, and in my own little dream world. In the background the French tape was mumbling on. Suddenly I found myself humming (this week's number one - Backstreet Boys). There I was humming away – not paying attention to anything – when there was a sudden BANG. Mr P-- had slammed down his pen and stormed out of the room, for what seemed to me to be for no apparent reason, but the whole class seemed to be staring at me . . .

*Faye Hatton*

BUT LOOKING AT IT, school was fun in a strange sort of way, and I liked to learn with my friends. I felt sorry for the children in the next few centuries who were facing the prospect of learning from computer all day at home in a polluted and bleak world, because their ancestors had been stupid enough to destroy it.

*Philippa Hemsley*

My school is brilliant.
         I think the teachers give you an excellent education.
         My school is very tidy and joyful.

*Samantha Stephen*

WALK UP THE GARDEN,
And out through the gate,
Quick, hurry up,
Don't be late!

As I walk down the lane
the bus drives past,
Like a big red dragon,
With people he's eaten,
Peering out of his sides!

I cross the road,
Look, there's my school,
Ahead I see the dragon bus,
Spitting out my friends!

We have all survived the journey to school,
So walk in through the gate,
Line up in our line,
Then into the dreaded school we go!

*Alice Scott-Jupp*

Flower *Hannah Sims*

LETTER TO PENPAL: To Simon. School's good. We do exciting things like Art and Technology. But there are some things that are a bit boring, like Maths and English. But I'm OK. I live in a big house with two cars and a garage, and a big brother and sister. Our garden is quite big too. We have five pets: they are two guinea pigs, two rabbits and a dog. My garden has a slope in it. I want to be a carpenter when I grow up, and make big things. I hope you write back and be my penpal.

*Joe Marks*

SCHOOL LIFE IN 1999 is very interesting, especially games lessons, in which we play good sports such as rugby, football and netball. Our DT lessons are good because we do woodwork and straw models. In our topics we do such things as the Tudors, India, and Health and Fitness. School days last from 8.50 to 15.25. In our schools we have house points for good work. Every time we get ten house points we get a sticker on our achievement card, and when we get ten stickers (100 house points) we get a pen with the name of the school on it given to us. My name is Henry Curr and I have written this so people in the future know what it was like at the turn of the millennium in Salisbury.

*Henry Curr*

*. . . interesting, indeed,*
*but fixed into a set routine.*
*Here is the school timetable,*
*from one of Henry's colleagues.*

*Friends Matthew Newman*

**MONDAY:** We come in from the play ground at 8.50 to do the register and then go to assembly until 9.30. We have English from 9.30 – 10.30, then we have break time. We go to Maths in different classes then we go to lunch in the hall. We have a spelling test after lunch in different classes. Then we have Science from 1.30 – 2.25, then we have break time, then more Science, then we go home at 3.25.

**Tuesday:** We come in from the play ground at 8.50, then do the register and then go to assembly. We do literacy hour from 9.30 – 10.30, then we go out to play. We come in and go to our Maths groups, then we go to lunch at 11.50. After lunch we have some new words for next Monday. We do Art from 1.30 – 2.25, then we go out to play, and come in and do more Art, then we go home.

**Wednesday:** We come in from the play ground to do the register and then go to assembly at 9.00 – 9.30. We do literacy hour from 9.30 – 10.30, then we have a break time. We go to our Maths groups at 10.45 – 11.45, then we go to lunch. We have Games from 1.20 – 2.20, then we have break time. Then we have Topic time, then we go home.

**Thursday:** We come in from the play ground to do the register and then go to assembly, then we go to the Library. Then we go out to play. We come in from play and go to our Maths groups. We come back and go to lunch. We come back and do silent reading, then we have literacy hour, then break time and then do Topic and then go home.

**Friday:** We come in and do the register, then we go to assembly. When we come back we have literacy hour, then we go out to play. We come in and go to our Maths group, then we go to lunch. Then we do music and then go out to play. Then we do D.T. and then go home.

*Edward Purvis*

Salisbury Cathedral *Joanna Raisbeck*

*School isn't always plain sailing.*

*Queasiness during Maths can be a setback . . .*

YESTERDAY I GOT UP FOR SCHOOL and got ready. I got to school at five to nine. We did the register. At five past nine we lined up to go to assembly. Afterwards we went back to our classroom and did map work. At half-past ten we went out to play. At ten forty-five I went to Maths. I missed some of my Maths because I wasn't very well. At eleven forty-five I went to lunch. I didn't eat all of it because I was ill. At lunchtime play I went into the medical room and Mrs X. told me that I was running just a minute ago and I wasn't. So I ran outside crying and told Mrs Y and Mrs Z, and they said find your best friend and ask if she would like to stay inside with me. After lunch we did more map work. At break time I played with my friends. After play we did music and watched a music video. At the end of the day I went home and my Step-Dad was there.

*Zoe Hardiman*

*And sometimes the problem is sheer embarrassment,*
*keenly felt by Godolphin girls on their way to a Cathedral service.*

As we lined up outside the house dressed up to the nines in our cloaks, blazers and boards, (a tradition that the school has unfortunately insisted that we keep,) I felt a hand on my back.

'Can I walk down next to you?' came the unavoidable question.

'Sure,' I replied and got in line behind two of my friends in front, ready for the trek down to Salisbury Cathedral.

As we set off down the hill, I prepared myself for the horrors yet to come. The stares from the foreigners visiting this delightful city, the snapping of cameras as we walk past groups on guided tours thinking that we were part of the deal, the astonished faces of drivers whose heads keep turning as the car drives away, swerves and eventually draws the attention of the driver back to the road.

I wasn't kept in suspense for very long, for as soon as we stepped out of the gate, a bus crammed with people drove slowly past and everyone on board turned round on their seats to stare at us as the bus continued around the corner. The girl standing next to me didn't seem to notice. She just kept on chatting away, her board crooked on her blond curls and her cloak done up on the wrong buttonholes. As nothing seemed to be happening,

I joined in the conversation going on between the two girls in front and the one next to me and was amazed to find myself at the bottom of the hill without having to hide myself or turn away even once!

However, the peace didn't last for long for as we stepped onto the pavement on the other side of the busy road a group of young boys came up the road towards us. I cringed inside and waited for the sniggers to begin. One, two three. . . there goes the first one: a tall dark lad burst out laughing and his desperate attempts to hide his laughter were to no avail until a sharp stare from the house mistress sent him scurrying on his way.

At last we reached the small dark passageway where we turned off past the multi-storey car park. It was unlikely that we were going to pass anyone, so I calmed down and was soon engrossed in another conversation between my friends. As some-one in front kicked an empty can on the floor, it set the resident dog for that area off into a series of howls and barks. As usual, all the younger years joined in with it and soon the whole passage way was filled with barks and howls of different varieties which only confused the poor dog even more!

When we left the dark passage-way, the worst part of the trip began. It was down this street, with houses on either side, that people would peek round their curtains and call to the others in the house, 'Come and look at this,' until the window was crammed with faces, big and small all staring with open mouths at the crocodile of children walking along their street. The first curtain that I saw twitch was one of the first ones that we passed. A small, dark-haired girl was looking at us in amazement and soon her mother was there, too. I hurried past and tried not to look at any of the other windows, but I knew that I wouldn't get away that easily. Soon a car drove past and the driver's face was classic. He was obviously foreign and stared at us in such a way that, even though I was slightly embarrassed, I had to laugh.

At last I saw the gates of the Cathedral Close and as we got into single file, I managed to sigh a sigh of relief, I'd made it! As we entered the Cathedral, we were greeted by smiles and pleasant words which calmed my agitated nerves and made me feel relaxed. Now all I had to face was the walk back!

*Sophie Hayes*

SCHOOL IS VERY COOL.

You can do loads of games.

You can do loads of work.

And games have very odd names.

*Jessica Fulford*

# AND A LOT OF
# NOISE!

Odeon Cinema, Salisbury *Melanie Rigg*

*Oh well, there's always the week-end to look forward to.*

AFTER A LONG AND BUSY SCHOOL WEEK, I enjoy going into Salisbury on a Saturday to unwind and enjoy myself with my friends.

My typical Saturday starts with having a lie in and then I catch the 11.30 bus from Landford to Salisbury. The bus travels all the way along the main road with an occasional detour through Whiteparish. It gets to the bus station at about 12.00.

Once I get off the bus I immediately notice the change in atmosphere; everything seems to be much faster and more urgent compared to the quiet, secluded country life in Landford. From the bus station I walk over to the Leisure Centre and have a game of football with my friends. We play for about an hour and then I walk back into the town.

In the town centre I get my lunch and go to the cinema with my mate who lives near me in Landford. Once the film has finished we both make our way over to the bus station and catch the next bus home. From the bus stop by the main road in Landford I have a 20-minute walk through the village to my home. I usually get in at about 4.00 in the afternoon.

Once I am home I will just lounge around in front of the TV and recover from my busy day.

*Stuart Dubber*

## Going into town has always been a favourite occupation.

DEAR RACHEL,

It is so beautiful in Salisbury during summer with all the colourful flowers at their best when the sun is shining. I went into town the other day with my friend Jo, and I was amazed at how beautiful it had become. There were flowers with colours that just spring out at you. There were little children playing their games on the field just by the cathedral.

The cathedral looks so big – the great towering glass windows with their pictures in coloured glass. But what I think spoils the view is the scaffolding which is around it, as the men are working to repair the stonework.

As Jo and I wandered around the town we decided to stop and have a look in the George Mall. We had forgotten how many popular shops there were there. Jo and I went into all of them (we had a disco that night so we bought clothes and shoes for that). Then we went to McDonald's for our lunch. I had a hamburger with all the fillings, some large fries and a large strawberry milkshake. To finish off the fabulous day we'd had we went to the cinema. Do you remember the one which looks like a Tudor house from outside, and is nice and cosy inside? We watched a great film called 'Twin Trouble' and scoffed ourselves silly with lots of sweets and popcorn. To top the day off we had a brilliant time disco dancing and showing off our new clothes.

Yours sincerely,

*Melanie Rainsley*

*Old George Mall Philippa Lawrence*

## All of which brings us round to the question of shopping.

I GO TO CLAIRES ACCESSORIES,
I buy lipstick and nail varnish,
Some red, some blue,
And some are even silver and gold.
Now I am going on the bus.
I shall have to run.
Oh no, there it goes without me.
I'd better walk home instead.

*Cloé Bartlett*

WOOLWORTHS IS A FAVOURITE SHOP,
I like Sainsbury's too.
Creme eggs, bread,
Veggy pies and chicken fries.
Forbuoys the newsagents shop
Sells sweets and chocolate bars.
B & Q has tools, paints, drills, hammers and bolts.
The Entertainer is my favourite shop.
Millions of toys, teddies, Action Men
And a lot of noise!

*Paul Willock*

*Market Square Milly Girling*

*And the noisiest shopping goes on in the Market Place.*

STRAIGHT AWAY

As you walk into the market
straight away you hear –
yelling, screaming, chatting.
As you walk into the market
straight away you smell –
fish, donuts, fruit.
As you walk into the market
straight away you see –
stalls, vans, trucks.
As I walk into the market I feel
excited – It's Saturday.

*Joel Friskney-Adams*

THE MARKET PLACE

The Market place
Is very noisy.
People are shouting, screaming,
        talking.
A strong smell of fish, donuts,
        olives and coffee fills the air.
It's full of colour because
        of flowers.
They hang in lovely hanging
        baskets,
In pots on the floor,
There are pansies, honeysuckles
        and tulips.
You can buy
Food, tools, petfood and clothes
But the best thing of all is –
The sweety stall.

*Ellen Heathcote*

## But some people are quite oblivious to the noise and bustle.

WHILE THE GUILDHALL SAT
LIKE A FRAME IN A PICTURE,
like a grandfather watching over
his children and grandchildren.
With the leafy green trees while
blowing gently shadowing the
forever moving shapes passing
from left to right and right to left,
forever moving.

There was a still and significant
gentle quietness about the stalls.

One could still hear the birds
above in the up and over
branches, giving this lovely
interesting market town and tourist trap a
sensation of nostalgia long felt.

Amidst all of this and the surrounding clutter,
two shoppers stood heads together, minds very
intent on what they were doing or the lack of it.

The silver-haired lady on the left pressed her
head forward, the pink cardigan standing out
quite distinctively and plucky, the flowing skirt
a strong contrast.

She seemed to have some interesting news to
tell, for the other woman had forgotten she was
in a hurry - the shopping could wait.

This listener with her quite soft white
see-through blouse loosely fitting but matching
the formal neat skirt.

They were greatly unaware of the significance
of their actions and of the hush that was going
on around them.

Their shopping forgotten, husband and family
did not matter at the precise moment. Soon
they knew what would be expected of them
rushing here and there and off home to the
family chores.

*Rose Hughes*

The Guildhall *Sarah Hatton*

### The range of merchandise is impressive.

SALISBURY'S SQUARE

Here I found in Salisbury's Square
A market full of underwear,
And don't forget the shoes and socks,
Women wearing golden locks,
Children running up and down,
Babies squealing round and round,
People shouting out things to buy,
And many sorts of shops nearby.

*Sophie Freemantle*

MARKET'S OVER and crowd-trapped individuals,
who scrutinised and fingered spilt merchandise,
escape to side-streets and expanding suburbia
or squeeze with freshly fattened plastic bags
through dusty country buses patiently waiting,
and bump between high hay-fields and thick hedges
back to their shopless villages of exile.

**But eventually it's time to take down the stalls,
and store them until next week . . .**

Market Square *Katie*

Market's over and pigeons whole or club-clawed,
banished to tile or cornice of observation,
descend silhouetted from heaven like polluted angels
to reclaim yet again their traditional parade ground.
They pause bemused a moment, then suddenly strut
in quest of supper, drumming air with foreheads.
Bandit starlings frustrate with snatching rushes.

Market's over and council-workers gaudy as parrots
grab crates of abandoned fruit and crumpled wrappings
and sacrifice them to jaws of voracious dust-carts.

Striped awnings hauled down like flags of the defeated.
Dropped steel poles attempt percussion band.
Doors slam on ponderous vans that seemed permanent.
They crawl away in quest of racing motorways
and cover the compass to depots quitted in mist.

Market's over and iron gates are padlocked
on subterranean toilets, and surrounding architecture
recovers its dignity and the square at last is quiet.

Moon cannon-balls fragile cathedral spire,
revealing to bulge-eyed fish and chip bay-windows
and classical columns of supercilious Town Hall
and boozy red facade of Ox Row Inn
and slim stiffs framed in glass of fashion store –
paving-stones trembling, lifting like trap-doors,
permitting a nocturnal resurrection
of centuries of markets buried here.

And secretly, unsensed even by constables,
forgotten characters with their cries and provender
circulate slowly in spectral cavalcade
and then, exhausted after long indolence
but sprinkled by galaxies of familiar stars,
*Peter Gillott*     they sink back inchmeal into silences and soil.

MOST DAYS:
Sun shining,
Cars driving,
People sitting,
Cars parking,
Dogs barking,
Skateboards flying,
Trees rustling,
People working,
Tarmac melting,
Windows open,
People sitting,
Bread baking,
Wind blowing,
People talking,
Men whistling,

Market days:
People shopping,
Awnings flapping,
Fish smelling,
Scaffolding banging,
Sun shining,
People shouting,
Vegetables spilling,
Trees rustling,
People running,
Doughnuts cooking,
People bargaining,
Bags filling,
People pushing,
Children squealing,

Funfair days:
Music thumping,
Rides spinning,
People retching,
Dodgems bumping,
Lights flashing,
Children crying,
Machinery grinding,
People screaming,
Noise blaring,
Drunks shouting,
Rides swooping,
People laughing,
Ferris wheels turning,
Rides whizzing,
People eating.

*In fact, the Market Place has three faces, depending on the day,*

Market Stalls *Shauni Burt*

*Miranda Garrett*

*Yes, the Market Place is where the Michaelmas Fair is held each autumn.*

EVERY YEAR A FAIR COMES TO TOWN. I went on the umbrellas. I was nearly sick. Also there's a cage where you stand up strapped to a cage, and then it starts to spin round and then it tips up, so one minute you're facing the sky and then you're facing the ground.

*Danielle Gray*

*The Fair was used by Thomas Hardy as the setting for a short story, but nothing as terrifying as this . . .*

'OH MY GOD!' was my first thought. We were all just staring at 'The Cage'. The latest ride at Salisbury Fair. As I was the most daring person amongst my group of friends, I wanted to go straight on.

As I had missed the fair last year, the suspense and excitement could wait no longer. The whole market square was filled with the dazzling array of lights, screaming voices and sounds which were all part of the thrill. All my friends wanted to join me apart from Jane. She really disliked these rides but I managed to persuade her in the end.

It was thirty minutes before we were at the front of the queue. Being so close up, the nerves and adrenaline started to kick in. The ride stopped and I thought there's no turning back. We walked on apprehensively and got strapped in opposite each other, which was even better. The music started, and I held on tight. Higher and higher we went, faster and faster it got. It wasn't too long before we were rotating practically upside down. It was great!

I could see Jane opposite me holding on really tightly and gripping with her feet. Nothing should have gone wrong because the G-force should have kept her in. It wasn't until we began to slow down that Jane started slipping. I didn't think much of it until she slipped lower and lower. I saw the horror in her eyes and her mouth opened but nothing came out. She just fell and fell, until finally she hit the ground. The ride did an emergency stop. By the time I got to her, crowds had gathered round her. I managed to get to her but realised she was dead.

*Lizzie Edwards*

## That was fiction. But what about this?

MY SISTER EMMA used to work in Debenhams. One day she came back as white as a sheet and shaking. My brothers and I joked around and said that she looked as if she had just seen a ghost! She gave us a harsh look and went running upstairs to her bedroom. She told us later on that evening, when she had calmed down a bit what had happened.

She was having one of her normal busy and hectic Saturdays in Salisbury on the menswear department of Debenhams. She was working behind the till when a young man of about twenty-five came in and asked if he could bring back a shirt he had bought from there last week. Emma took the shirt and asked if he wanted a refund or to change it for a different size. He said he wanted to change it for a bigger size. There were not any shirts in the right size left on the shop floor so Emma went down to the store room which she does quite often. But this time she said it felt different. It seemed as if another person was down there, but she knew there wasn't anyone there because the door was locked when she had got down there.

She walked cautiously in and as she was looking for the right sized shirt she saw this bright light with this ghost-like headless man walking towards her. She just froze. It walked closer to her and then it suddenly vanished. She grabbed the shirt and ran back to the shop floor. She was shaking like mad as she gave the man his shirt and went to go and sit down. One of the other sales assistants went over to see if she was all right. Emma explained what had happened. Some of the other sales assistants felt brave enough to go and have a look. But they couldn't find anything. There were no clues that a ghost had been there. Emma got the rest of the day off and someone gave her a lift home. She lay on her bed all that afternoon. She did not want to talk to anyone because she was so shaken up.

No one has seen the ghost since. Is it still there????

*Hannah Fisher*

Alison Hogg

AS WELL AS THE ENJOYMENT OF THE ACTUAL EVENTS, there is also a lot of fun during the preparation of the day. I remember when I was about four or five helping to build the very first dragon for the play in next door's garden. It was made out of paper mache', mounds of cloth and two beach balls for eyes! I have also taken part in the procession and been a dancer. I always love joining in, and everyone always seems to have a good time.

St George's Day is a very popular event in Salisbury. It brings a lot of the community together, and almost everyone takes part in one small way or another. To me, it marks the coming of a new season, as it is one of the first outdoor events of the year in Salisbury. It is very much a family day.

I really enjoy St George's Day, and feel privileged to live in a city where it is celebrated so well. Who knows, perhaps it will still be going by the next millennium?

*Daisy Drury*

Market Walk
*Hannah Keegan Podger*

*Other historical fears have a happier ending.*

I COULD SMELL THE AROMA OF COFFEE as I grew nearer Michael Snell's. Usually I can't stand the smell, but this time something else made me feel sick; it was the thought of dancing in front of the mayor and the cameras of 'Songs of Praise' and everyone else who turned up for St George's Day.

I stood waiting for the rest of the dancers in my black trousers, very loud silk shirt and flashy tie. But I did not feel embarrassed to wear these things. Compared to everyone else around Michael Snell's I was very under-dressed!

I was fascinated by the tall jesters on stilts and the medieval costumes. Each costume must have taken weeks to make.

As I stood watching all of this the giants came around the corner. They gave me the fright of my life! My friends and I were trying to remember the three names of them, only succeeding to remember St Christopher, the most commonly known, and I think the best because of the heroic stories about him. I walked up to the giants and couldn't figure out how the person inside the woman giant could see.

It was time to start the parade to the market square. The mayor walked first, along with the dignitaries, after them the giants and Hobnob the horse. Then there was the long line of cubs, brownies, dancers and actors. Even though we were a small part in the festivities I still felt important. As we got to the market square I prepared to dance to a song from 'Five Guys named Moe'. My stomach felt so knotted it was hard to swallow, but I managed to smile throughout the dance. As the dance ended I felt sad that my part was over.

After our dance we sat at the front and saw the highlight of the production, the performance of 'St George and the Dragon'.

St George's day has been marked on the calendar for many, many years, still catching eyes of the public every time. I look forward to the next one!

*Emilia Williams*

*And it is not only in Salisbury*
         *that springtime is celebrated with a fair.*

WHY I LIKE
THE CUCKOO FAIR

The Cuckoo fair
Is always there.
It has been for
Hundreds of years.
It used to be huge
But now it's small,
It used to be fun,
But now it's uncool.
There's a May Pole with
Dancers, and hundreds of
Crafters all selling their wares.
There's a coconut shy
Which is there in the dry.
And a train
Which runs in the rain.
Animals to feed,
Donkeys to ride,
A colour maze which
Is never there.
That's why I like the
Cuckoo Fair.

*David Barnett*

CUCKOO FAIR

Cuckoo Fair comes once a year,
To a quiet village here.
People come from near and far,
To hear the people sing 'la la'.
Stalls and games can be seen,
Just pop over before it's been.
Little girls and little boys sing and dance,
Why not come and see them prance.
Downton becomes a lively place,
When people see the ferrets race.
'Roll up, Roll up!' the games hosts cry,
Smell those nice burgers fry.
The sun is high and the day is bright,
Why not come over here for the night.
The barn dance and band will entertain,
And they go on despite the rain.
Once again the Cuckoo Fair is gone,
But another year won't seem so long.

*Tracy Gooding*

# WILL THERE
# STILL BE FIELDS
# AND TREES?

........................

*So it's time to explore Downton -*

*not far from Salisbury. In fact . . .*

IF YOU STAND

at the top

of the cathedral

on a clear day

and the right

direction

you could see

Downton.

**Luke Pickard**

*True, but rather difficult to achieve.*

*The other way round is easier....*

*Besides the school,*
*Downton has other amenities.*

The bakery's cakes

are really nice,

Co-op sells food at a

reasonable price.

The leisure centre

gives you lots to do,

While the birds in

the park sing

loudly to you.

*Nicky Marchant*

I AM SITTING AT MY DESK enjoying the view from a window in a mobile at Downton School.

In the distance I can see a big, green hill that looks as though it goes right up to the sky. On the top and round the sides there are clusters of trees, of which you can just see the dark green leaves.

A bit closer I can see more fields that farmers use to graze sheep, cows and horses. A bright yellow field is filled with rape seed, which is used for its oil, and I can see a vivid red field overflowing with poppies.

In the foreground there are Year Sevens doing P.E. - rounders and athletics. You can immediately see who enjoys it and who doesn't. I personally don't, as it's too tiring and I find it too much hard work on a summer's day.

If I go to the other side of the mobile I can see our school: a substantial building but rather a drab place, where it depresses most people to be in.

If I strain my eyes I can see Salisbury Cathedral that is so distant it could be in a dream. If there is a mist it looks almost ghost-like. Salisbury has quite a lot of medieval buildings but the cathedral is by far the most magnificent.

I love the countryside, and I wonder if it will be the same when you are reading this. I wouldn't want you to miss out on all this.

*Samantha Albery*

## *And there is the Downton Countryside Walk.*

### WALKING DOWN THE VILLAGE,

Walking down the village
Along the Borough, past
Lode Cottage, Grannies
Knitting, drinking
In the Bull,
Nodding to everyone at the village
Gathering - Bill, Sue, Toby, Candy, and the rest.

Talking. Chatting. People
Outside the White Horse.

Do some shopping in the Co-op, buying
Opalfruits for my walk.

Down the track,
Over the bridge,
Walking, looking, listening -
Noticing different sounds.
Tannery smells floating
Over the river,
Nearer to me.

Cuckoo! Cuckoo!
Over there.
Under that tree,
Near that house.
Take a picture,
River splashing,
Young boys fishing in the
Slow running stream.
In the river, bigger children
Jumping in; the best way for
Entertainment.

Walking slowly
Along the
Long river bank, people
Kayak by.

**Corinne Gatehouse**

*But here, as elsewhere, village life seems threatened.*

THERE USED TO BE A SHOP ON MOOT LANE where I used to get all my sweets from until it got knocked down and turned into three houses. I wasn't very happy when this happened, because from then on I had to go all the way down the road to the shop. There is a meadow at the bottom of Greenacres where I used to go minnow fishing with my jar and net, but now people have bought it so you are not allowed in it any more.

Rabbit Burrow *Lucy Hill*

*Heidi Hitchens*

*The nagging fear that the new millennium will see a countryside spoiled has inspired several pithy and sensitive poems.*

I WONDER . . .

What life will be like in the
21st century?
Will there still be fields
and trees?
Will sparkling rivers still flow
to the seas?
Will there still be hawks
and kites?
And animals that hunt in
the night!
Will there be dainty plants that
move in the breeze?
Will there be daffodils with big
green leaves?
Will migrant birds still spread
their wings?
Will mornings wake when
church bells ring?
I hope this is what life will be
like in the 21st century.

*Annie Samuels*

## THE PEACEFUL AND TRANQUIL WOOD

In a quiet and desolate, dark wood, thousands
      of creatures lie unseen.
A haven for snails, woodlice and ants, where
      for years they have been.
Trees have been hollowed out,
Roots have been uplifted,
Logs have been upturned.
Creatures have been busy making
      homes in trees, bushes, and ferns.
Leaves have been used for dens,
Moss has been used for nests,
Twigs have been used for props to keep
      everything looking at its best.
Further in the wood badgers and foxes
hunt, leap and run.
While back at the den the cubs await
While playing and snoozing in
      the sun.
Please keep this beautiful wood
      peaceful and tranquil,
So that my descendants are truly thankful.

*Jenna Copp*

*Alison Hogg*

## NEAR THE LITTLE TOWN OF MINE

*This is the beautiful countryside, near the little
town of mine . . .*
Trees are a fresh, leafy green
Grass swaying like a bed of green sea
Daffodils are bright yellow like a ray of sun
Poppies are as red as dripping blood
Bluebells tingle and shimmer with blue
And snowdrops are as white as snow.

*Is this the beautiful countryside, near the little
town of mine . . .*
Trees will be replaced with concrete buildings
Grass will be covered in tar
Daffodils will be changed into factories
Poppies will stand as iron figures
Bluebells will lie as scattered litter
And snowdrops will no longer be.

*Ella Scott*

*For those who live in Salisbury or
its suburbs, the rich surrounding
countryside provides a
welcome escape.*

### HARNHAM HILL

I like the hill because there's lots of exciting things
to see and hear. I like the steps we climb up and
run up too. There's hills all around the actual hill.
I've got a favourite hill that I run down. There are
steps that I run up or walk up. The hill is one of
my best places in Harnham. There's lots of
animals there, but there's mostly squirrels. In the
autumn I like going up and kicking the leaves
about. From my bedroom window I can see all
the different colours shining amongst the trees.
The trees are big and strong and make me think
of giants having a chat. The wood makes me think
a lot about things. The leaves are like the little
mice running up and down the giant and skipping
in the giant's garden.

*Emma Cole*

Old Mill *Lucy Phipps*

MY FAVOURITE WALK IS OVER THE TOWN PATH.
I can see the old mill with the ducks outside, and children having great fun in the water on a hot summer's day. As I walk on I see our cathedral towering above everything. There are cows and sheep on either side of the path which my little brother likes to see. Bicycles keep passing by jingling their bells to warn us they are coming. It often makes me jump! Soon I come to a bridge that links to Elizabeth Gardens, with trees and swans and children in the park, and suddenly lots of noise! The town path is a very special walk.

*Rebecca Gorringe*

Salisbury's green places are magic.
Please don't take **them** away.
Let the children of the future
Enjoy them in the same way.

*Isabel Spring*

I AWOKE TO THE SOUND OF BIRDSONG. It was my day for looking after Richard and Jonathan, my grandsons, whilst their parents were at work. They brought bows and arrows with them to play with, a weapon from the iron ages or before, the arrows were not so dangerous as then. We walked to Bishopdown Green so that they could shoot them, it made me think of the modern weapons being used in Kosovo at this time. Then we walked to the new cycle path, it had taken us 18 years to get this path constructed so that the children could cycle to school at Laverstock from Bishopdown. It was hazardous crossing the road at the crematorium, the cars go so fast trying to beat the traffic lights it's a wonder the children crossing to school don't get their bikes whipped from them whilst waiting in the middle. Once over the road and under the railway arch it was a different atmosphere altogether, lovely green meadows and trees, at the bridge two swans were beginning to build their nest, the river was clear and we saw some fair sized minnows. It was so lovely and peaceful

and in the distance we could see a helicopter circling around, the blackthorn was out in the hedgerow and a tree with two clumps of mistletoe growing at the top. On the way home we decided to collect some tadpoles from their cousin's pond.
It turned out quite warm and with the window open at teatime my husband and I were able to eat our tea to the most beautiful sound of a blackbird singing. A lovely ending to the last day of March 1999.

*Mrs C.A. Thompson*

*For some residents,*
*of long standing or recently arrived,*

MY HOUSE AT LIMPERS HILL stands a stone's throw from the cottage where my grandfather grew up. When I walk to town, I see the window from which he jumped as he ran away to sea at the age of twelve. He set off on his adventures down the same narrow lane that leads to Mere. His mother was left to wait 'under the elm' for his return.

Limpers Hill was elm country when my husband, Bernard, and I built our house here over thirty years ago. Those tall trees dominated the landscape. There were two huge elms in the field beyond our boundary and many more in the hedgerows. Today the view is different. The elms are gone - victims of Dutch Elm Disease - and they are not encouraged to make a come-back. Any suckers that push their way up through the hedges are cruelly hacked away by trimming machines.

Another import has changed this corner of Wiltshire. Meadows are ploughed and planted with maize – corn as 'high as an elephant's eye' . Now I walk through rows of rotting stalks where once golden king-cups spread themselves along water ley-lines, and careful searching revealed the pink bell-flower of the delicate water avens. The droves, once lined with purple vetch and ragged-robin, are churned to mud by contractors working to fixed prices and little time to take care. But thankfully, bluebells still flower in Charnage Wood, wild garlic blankets the hedgerows like snow, and banks of cow-parsley narrow the road.

Grandfather returned to Limpers Hill after five years sailing the world. Later he moved into town and settled at Old Hollow. Now, following that hidden circuitry which links generations together, I am doing likewise. Bernard has built a new house in Old Hollow - on the site of Grandfather's cottage.

*Adrienne Howell*

*living in the south Wiltshire countryside seems an unqualified delight.*

My House *James Vaughan*

IN DURRINGTON
there are friends to play with.
There are lots of cars,
there are rabbits and guinea pigs,
and lots of different animals
to have fun with.
There is a big sports centre
to go to in Amesbury.
You do roller-blading there.
There are lots of books to read too.
At Old Sarum you see lots of planes.
And at night the stars come out
with the moon shining in the sky.
And then I go to sleep.

*Hannah Sims*

## WILTSHIRE WOODS

The hand of nature
Paints with ease
The changing landscape;
Grows the farmer's corn;
Sends the hungry pigeon
Flapping through the trees,
Gives sound to the hunter's horn.
Conducts the gentle murmurs
Of the bees
Sharing with flowers on a sunny morn.

*Martyn Jones*

## MY VILLAGE: LANDFORD

Our village is not very old,
It has a certain charm.
The New Forest is next door,
And so is many a farm.

The old village school stood
on a nearby hill,
But the plague claimed
many lives,
The church still stands there
at the top,
The only thing which
survives.

There's always something
going on,
And things to see and do.
Two village halls see lots
of fun,
For children and adults too.

There's usually sport on the
village rec.,
And a playground for one
and all.
The mobile library comes
around,
To set up its weekly stall.

The post office and
village shops
Form a chat and
gossip point.
They catch up on the
village news,
When they buy the
Sunday joint.

I have been here all my life,
I hope I'll always stay,
I love the timeless
village life,
In each and every way.

*Belinda Jacob*

# I WOULDN'T
# WANT TO LIVE IN
# A CITY

........................

*The small towns of South Wiltshire
also come in for praise.*

Bulford Kiwi *Julia Blomquist*

AMESBURY WAS ONCE A QUIET HAMLET,
With dusty village by-ways,
But now it's bustling with many shops,
By-passed by tarmac highways.

I have lived in Amesbury all my life.
It is a lovely place to be.
The view from my bedroom is of the town,
And beyond that is the free country.

The woodland and the rivers,
Where the wildlife abounds.
Beyond that is the spacious Salisbury Plains,
Where the fox flees in terror from the hounds.

The burial mounds are scattered far and wide.
The sheep graze under tall beech trees.
Then beyond on the twilight horizon,
The powerful Stonehenge you can see.

But back to the noise of traffic and market,
To the life of a busy town,
To the noise of the children playing at school,
To the roar of the fighters at Boscombe Down.

There are many lovely towns in Wiltshire,
Many beautiful areas to see.
But of all the places I have visited,
My favourite is still Amesbury!!

*Katie Luxton*

Stone Circle *James Davies*

MERE CHURCH TOWER

Four pinnacles on high –
Grey against the sky.
Up comes the sun – behold –
Four flags of gold!
What a delight.
I, from my home, can see
(When sun and wind are right)
This splendid sight,
Oh lucky me!

*Miss B.M. Naylor*

*But no-one would deny that village life has its problems. For most the advantages outweigh the drawbacks.*

New Forest *Emma Leighfield*

MANY PEOPLE WOULD LIKE TO LIVE IN A VILLAGE or near the New Forest, whereas some have lived there all their lives, and may not appreciate it as much. The facilities in some small villages are very poor: most just have the basic – small shop, post office, recreation grounds, church, bakery, primary school, public house, and perhaps a farm shop; but although they have all of these food shop there are no leisure facilities.

As my village is in between Salisbury and Southampton, it is easy for me to get into either town by bus, which costs me £3 for a return, so if I wanted to go to the cinema, it would cost me £6. There are other leisure facilities here, too. Near me there are about four public swimming pools.

In a big city there would be more things and you wouldn't have to go far, but the city is very crowded and noisy. At least in a village you do not have to leave it if you like the quiet and peaceful areas and you can easily get into town. If you live in a town, however, you have the noise all the time.

*Laura Goss*

ALDERBURY IS A PLEASANT VILLAGE but there is little to do for young people. There are various clubs and things like guides, scouts and football, but they don't appeal to very many teenagers because they don't take place every night, and groups like these are different from just going ice skating.

In Alderbury we have a canal that is not suitable for anything. If it was clean then you could swim in it and have rowing, canoeing and sailing on it, although it's a little enclosed so it's not that windy for sailing. The canal, at the present time, is totally disgusting, dirty and dangerous, with lots of little twigs and things in it. It's also unhealthy, because of the dirt and rubbish. It would be really interesting and many activities could take place if someone would put money into it and make it useful. Walks could be planned around the canal because it's in the middle of a wood.

We do have a recreation ground but it's mainly aimed at younger children.

We have some tennis courts, but they are some way away from where most teenagers live – it's wearing out just walking up there, let alone playing tennis.

We have a Spar shop and a post office, but they don't sell penny sweets any more and the prices are going up all the time. Alderbury has two pubs as well.

I have a friend in Alderbury so I can go out if it's sunny, and sit and chat. There are lots of new estates so people are always moving in and out all the time.

In Alderbury many houses have gardens of a reasonable size so you can play in them.

When driving through the village it's very pretty, with lots of flowers and it's clean. We also have a lovely community.

*Rachel Rainsley*

I LIVE IN A COUNTRY VILLAGE CALLED BRITFORD on the outskirts of Salisbury. Opposite my house there's a wood, which is actually a heron sanctuary, and out of my bedroom window I can look out over the water meadows.
My parents say that I'm lucky to live in a village like Britford but I find it boring. I must admit that the scenery is beautiful, and I can understand why people come and look at it, but there's nothing to do apart from walk round and look at fields, woods and animals.

The city isn't too far away but I have to walk to it most of the time because my parents won't drive me there much because of the traffic problems. The city is about a 30-45 minute walk from my house, and there are only a few things to do there. I can go shopping which I love, I can go to the cinema, or there is a swimming pool but it keeps closing. There's a library and a playhouse but I don't really like them much.

It is rumoured that a leisure complex is planned. This will have a bowling alley, a better cinema and a swimming pool, which will give us more to do, so I really hope they do build it.

Even though I find the village boring I wouldn't want to live in a city.

*Amanda Cooper*

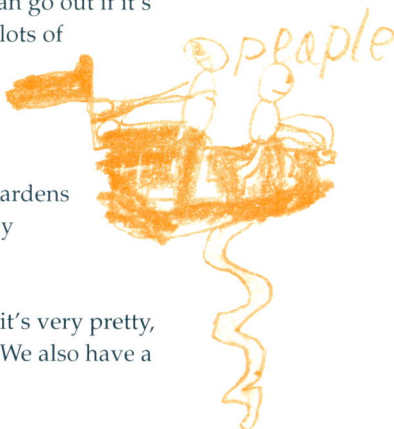

Play Field *David*

> *And here is another thoughtful view of Alderbury,*
> *balanced and fair, but full of foreboding.*

I HAVE LIVED IN ALDERBURY ever since I can remember, and all my best moments have happened there. Salisbury is the closest town and is linked to Alderbury by a main road, which means that the country-side around Alderbury is being threatened by new housing developments. Alderbury has a good selection of facilities, including pubs, tennis courts, halls, social groups, a church and a primary school. It is a very friendly village with a good mix of old and new resi-dents, who are all catered for. There is a good bus service, so I can see friends regularly.

Over the last few years, Alderbury has had many new housing estates and houses being built, and I am worried about the effects on the village and the countryside. In the village there are only limited numbers of people that can use the facilities and get into the small church, halls and primary school. So with more people competition for places will grow. To solve one problem of overcrowding in the guide

group they have produced a second troop. This is a good idea but it has its limits, especially on space.

With more people moving into Alderbury there is the usual problem of traffic, making it dangerous and polluted. They have put up a 30 mph speed limit in Alderbury after a lot of campaigning, but it is not being enforced, so some people take no notice, which is a problem.

Another problem which a larger population has is vandalism and anti-social behaviour towards other people and property. There is a small police station which is managing, but I fear that it might not be able to cope soon. There are a lot of old buildings in Alderbury, and with the new buildings it might not look very good.

With the countryside being destroyed, animals are being forced out, and they either end up on the road or die out. There is no vet or organisation locally to help this, so the problem just grows.

There are some good things about the village growing, which are that there will be new friends and people to meet. Another good thing is that the small businesses may expand, making Alderbury wealthier and possibly a nicer place to live. Also people may bring new ideas and organisations, so there will be more things happening and things to do. There are good things but they do not outweigh the bad.

I have decided to write about my village because next to my house there was a gravel pit where we used to play. Now this has been turned into a housing estate with people who I still do not know. Also there is a plot of wild ground which has been sold, and planning permission for a new house has just gone through. There are a lot of fields between Alderbury and Salisbury and I fear it will be turned into town and we will soon merge with Salisbury.

*Michael Sparrow*

# IT WOULD BE
MUCH BETTER
IF....

..........................

THERE'S REALLY ONLY ONE PROBLEM, TRAFFIC. To be honest I don't think anyone likes the traffic that rumbles through the centre day and night. It poses an immediate threat to safety. What I would really like to see in the new millennium is a traffic-free centre, where children can enjoy themselves without fear of being 'mown down' by passing traffic.

*William Ibbotson*

*Several of Michael's concerns have been voiced by many contributors, from town and city.*
*Take traffic and transport, for example . . .*

PUBLIC TRANSPORT: I need something that not just I have to rely on, but a system that others could benefit from too, taking people into Salisbury to work or just to shop at the weekend, as well as during the week.

*Zarah Chappell-King*

SALISBURY CITY CENTRE HAS RECENTLY BEEN PEDESTRIANIZED. So it has made shopping easier and more safe. There are also plans for a park and ride, which would take even more traffic out of Salisbury. For as long as I can remember, there has been talk of a by-pass to take traffic out of the city, but it has never gone ahead. I am not sure that it ever will.

*Katie Allen*

MAYBE THEY COULD USE TRAMS for a better, faster service. I hope that you, a school pupil in the future several generations after me, will have hassle-free journeys to school.

*Thomas Glyde*

# TRAFFIC

**T**oo many lorries, too many vans.

**R**oads congested, no real plans.

**A**ccidents, road rage, gridlocked town.

**F**aster, faster run them down.

**F**umes making holes in the ozone layer.

**I** don't think they really...

**C**are.

*Louis Harbison*

Car **William Creech**

KEEPING SALISBURY GREEN AND CLEAN

Times are changing,
Things rearranging.
Old people moaning,
Young people phoning.
Litter is growing,
Rubbish is blowing
In every street –
Which used to be neat.
There is a solution
To all this pollution.
Leave the car,
Town's not that far.
It pays to be Green,
So keep Salisbury Clean.

*Lloyd Perry*

Elizabeth Gardens *Florence Ellis*

## SALISBURY THE OLD AND THE NEW

To a senior citizen it is beautiful,
To a teenager it is ugly.

To a senior citizen the night
clubs are noisy,
To a teenager they are a
drinking hole.

To a senior citizen the parks
are peaceful,
To a teenager they are a giant
playground.

To a senior citizen the cinema
is memories,
To a teenager it is packed full
of action.

To a senior citizen the skate park
is an accident waiting
to happen,
To a teenager it is another
daring challenge.

To a senior citizen it is **new**
and developing,
To a teenager it is **old** and
ageing by the minute.

That was the old and the new.

*James Beeson Gould*

## A LETTER TO THE COUNCIL

Salisbury District Council,
32 Endless Street Salisbury.

Dear Sir / Madam,
I am 14 years old and I feel that there is
nothing for young teenagers to do in and
around Salisbury.

I think that it would be much better if an
amusement park was built. There are plenty of
areas big enough, e.g. : The fields behind the
cattle market on the Netherhampton Road; the
water meadows near the Leisure Centre; the
fields near the chalk pit in Harnham. And
instead of building new houses on the fields near
Odstock Hospital, that land is big enough to
hold an enormous amusement park.

If a small seaside town like Poole can cope with
having a large amusement park like Tower Park,
with bowling, a swimming pool and flumes,
multi-screen cinema, gambling arcades, a few
restaurants and even a supermarket, then I think
Salisbury (with its many tourists), can manage to
come up with something.

I'm not suggesting that we are short of super-
markets or restaurants because we aren't, but
what I am saying is that Salisbury is boring for
children of my age (14 upwards). If there was an
amusement park with a decent swimming pool
(the nearest good one is at Sandy Balls), an ice-
rink (the nearest are Swindon and Basingstoke,
and they're not exactly brilliant!) Salisbury
would attract even more tourists than usual! If
there was some kind of amusement park in
Salisbury it would keep all the children (all ages)
occupied. It would also keep more kids off
the street.

I honestly think that you should take this idea
into consideration.

Many thanks
Yours faithfully,

*Daisy Prangnell*

*Another recurring complaint is the lack of facilities for young people, and its consequences.*

Elizabeth Frink Sculpture *Grace Travis*

MY THOUGHTS AND
FEELINGS ABOUT SALISBURY

Salisbury City,
It looks quite pretty,
It's clean and tidy,
I think its okay,
But it's not the best.
It's aimed at the old,
I think that anyway.
It's full of art,
Statues and historic buildings.
I think it needs to be changed
To the now.
I think it looks like something,
From the 1850s.
I would really like more
Things for kids.
The swimming pool is
really un-cool.
We need something like,
Flumes, and rapids too.
I don't like the Close,
The people in it like to boast.
They're all so posh,
and full of dosh.
I think the Cathedral
Will never get finished,
Because once they're done
One side they'll have to
Do the other.
I live near Elizabeth Gardens.
It's just like it was mine.
I play almost every sport on it.
I love all the rivers.
My favourite street
is Water Lane,
Because I live there.
The lady up the lane is a pain,
Because she always complains.
Salisbury's getting bigger,
With lots of new shops.
I hope they don't overdo it,
As I like Salisbury a lot.

*Craig Podger*

## SALISBURY: MY POINT OF VIEW

I think Salisbury is more of an old people's or pensioner's place to live. Apart from the shops there is not much for young people to do. If we go into town every weekend we will be bored stupid!

I think that there should be a large building on the edge of town with a bus stop, a multi-activity scheme and at least one Macdonald's or Burger Bar. If the Council did build this it should contain some sports courts with basketball hoops, tennis nets and a range of other equipment; an indoor skate park with seats for spectators; a cinema; a cyber café and a swimming pool. It should also have a disco or club with at least one disco a fortnight for 14-16 year olds.

If this doesn't happen I think they should, as a minimum, extend the existing skateboard and basketball courts across from Salisbury College and put more benches around all the parks. The theatre should put on a programme of events more suitable for teenagers. A range of active workshops would be brilliant. There is a lack of part-time employment for young people. Apart from working in a supermarket or other kind of shop, there's not a lot of opportunity at the moment.

In Salisbury there are far too many pubs. It just causes vandalism and fights - particularly at the weekends. I think that instead of spreading out all the pubs, the Council should select a suitable area to have five or six large pubs and clubs close together so if young people want to go on a drinking binge they can so long as they stay within the area. This would cut down a lot of problems for local people who often have to put up with drunken behaviour at closing time. Those pubs which have an historic value, should focus on older people, and could perhaps offer a range of other services like accommodation.

*Miranda Flood*

*Alison Hogg*

SALISBURY ON THE WHOLE IS A FRIENDLY PLACE.
But beneath the surface this is hardly the case.
The constant traffic jams are enough to drive anyone mad,
And as for amusement - well, that's really bad!
If you want a drink there's 105 pubs,
But if you're under-18 you're basically stuffed!
The cinema's fun but what a price to pay.
They must think we've got pounds saved away!
For tourists there's the Cathedral, the market place too,
But it even costs you ten pence to go to the loo!
The swimming pool is boring, the leisure centre's too.
And, other than that, there's not a lot to do.
If you want to have fun, the train's your best bet,
A ticket away... the best idea yet!
But having said this there's nothing I can do.
My parents chose Salisbury which means I'm here too!
Perhaps when I am older I may appreciate it more,
For here in the city there are pensioners galore!!!

*Gemma Skelton*

## *A darker side of city life emerges too.*

WHEN YOU ARRIVE AT THE TUNNEL-OUTSIDE-THE-LIBRARY you immediately become intimidated. Emerging from each side of the dismal tunnel are homeless people playing out of tune musical instruments that clash with each other. In the case of the even less fortunate people they huddle a flea-bitten thin dog whilst shivering in a blanket that has been moth-eaten. People stay as far away from them as possible and look at them as if they were diseases – which is sad.

*Katherine Goddard*

SALISBURY IN DAYLIGHT LOOKS A PLEASANT QUIET CITY, but by night it's a different story. When they let the animals out, the streets turn into a jungle, the pubs turn into dens and the punters into lions. Yet even the jungle is more civilized than Salisbury by night . . . Salisbury isn't all bad, though. It is just a shame that a few people have to spoil a whole city.

*Amy Albery*

Poultry Cross *Hannah May Purkiss*

# DRUNKARDS EVERYWHERE

Drunkards, drunkards everywhere,

The council doesn't seem to care!

Dossers, dossers living rough,

Why is life for them so tough?

Life in Salisbury is so bad,

Thats why people seem so sad!

*William Marks*

# I RECALL WITH
## FONDNESS

..........................

View from my bedroom window *Simon Willi*

## *The appalling plight of the homeless*
### *leads us to think of life in our own homes....*

I RECALL WITH FONDNESS, a sunny afternoon in the late 1970s. I would have been about ten years old; my friend Julia and I were doing our homework in her garden. I used to like going to her house as she kept guinea pigs and I was only allowed a goldfish!

The topic for her homework, and chat (more chat than homework), was 'my life in the year 2000'. We had to predict how, through technology, our lives would change, and what 'gizmos and gadgets' would be in use.

I had always wanted a dog (my parents refused but gave in when I was 13), and through watching too many episodes of 'Doctor Who' on a Saturday evening, thought that by the year 2000 we would all be walking something along the lines of 'k9' (a metal box robotic dog on wheels)!

I also imagined that we would all be waited on hand and foot by robots who would do everything and that we wouldn't have to lift a finger (other than to reach for the zapper)!

I imagined that we would no longer have to cook (or wash up afterwards) as we would take a tablet for breakfast, that would taste of say - bacon and eggs; another tablet for lunch and then another for dinner, all tasting of whatever dish we happened to fancy at the time. I blame this theory on Roald Dahl and his book *Charlie and the Chocolate Factory*.

Many changes have happened in the 20th century and not unlike my predictions. I wonder how my daughter, Lauren, would predict the 22nd century and if any of her predictions will become reality. Only her children and their children will know.

I have a house, a job and a family of my own (and guinea pigs)... I could never have imagined that!

*Lindsay Newell*

IT WAS A QUARTER TO 10 IN THE MORNING, I awoke to the sound of my little brother SHOUTING at me to wake up. So I got up and got dressed and went downstairs to get my usual breakfast (Kellogg's Frosties). I watched TV and played fetch with my dog (Fly). Then it was time for the party - all of my Dad's side of the family and friends would be there, it was my Great Grandma's birthday. It was on Saturday the 6th of March at 4.00 pm at Gloucester House, which is at Hudson Road, in the Day Room. At the party I really enjoyed myself and there were lots of people there I didn't know.

My Great Grandma is called Lillian Weston, and she is 90 years old.

I stayed with my cousins most of the time at the party. We began to eat at about 4.30 pm, I had a lot to eat. I went into the toilets and pulled what I thought was the light switch but it was the emergency alarm for the elderly residents. When everyone had gone home we helped to clear up and then sat in my Great Grandma's flat talking for a while.

I got home at 9.00 pm and went to bed while mum and dad watched a film called 'Ace Ventura When Nature Calls' on the television.

*Richard Thompson*

My Rabbit Buzz *Alex Watterston*

STEPS LEAD DOWN TO A SLIGHTLY OVERGROWN LAWN, to the left of which is a hedge which separates our neighbour's garden from ours. On the lawn stands a barbeque built from large white bricks. To the left of that is a wendy house in which my sister and I had many interesting times, but which we now use to store all the dog and rabbit foods.

*Chris Mustow*

## A DAY IN THE LIFE OF ALEX

In the morning I get off the top bunk of my bunk-beds and watch television for ten minutes. I have my breakfast and get dressed. I brush my teeth and after that I say good-bye to Dad when he goes to work. Then I go downstairs and outside to feed my rabbit named Buzz. He is white with black spots on. Next I go to school. My teacher is called Mr Hamilton and is 43 years old. After that I go to my child minders for two hours and then I go home.

Please could you send a nine-year-old boy back in time to be my brother because I'm a lonely child - the address is Kingsland Road - in the year 2000. Thank you.

*Alex Watterston*

Hudsons Field *Kristi-Lee Wright*

THE HORSESHOE GREEN

**H**ousing estates all over
the place,
**A**round the houses is
open space.
**R**unning around the
horseshoe green,
**N**o grass where everyone
else has been.
**H**urrying home in time
for tea,
**A**ll the lads will be back
at three.
**M**any balls have been lost...
few are found!

*James Ockenden*

... WELL-MOWN LAWN, a summer house, and of course a goal for me and my little brother to play football in. I can also see the bare earth patches in the lawn which mark the penalty spot and goal mouth.

*Tim Hodson*

## But football is not our only diversion from school, work, or home.

IF YOU ASKED MOST PEOPLE what Salisbury means to them, they might reply 'The Cathedral' or 'Stonehenge,' 'The shops,' or, sighing wearily, 'School.' But Salisbury could only ever mean one thing to me: jumping up and down on a Saturday morning screaming 'Go on, Salisbury!' What sport could this be? Football? Rugby? Tennis, maybe? No. I'm talking utmost speed, strength, stamina, commitment and great team spirit. I'm talking Athletics!

O.K. So Salisbury Athletics Club may not be the most successful or impressive club, and O.K., so we may have been relegated to division four in the Women's Southern League, but that doesn't mean it's not top of MY league!

The highlights of my week come on Tuesday and Thursday evenings when I forget all the pressures of everyday life and meet my friends at Salisbury track. You find everyone down there, from the tall, skinny high jumper, to the short, sturdy shot putter; the county pentathlete champion to the plump try-hard who always loses; but I know I have something in common with all of them – my devotion to athletics.

The little children sprint round with endless supplies of energy while the veterans jog slowly round and round the track. The throwers lift weights and the jumpers do ballistic drills, while the endless supply of cheerful coaches encourage them and spur them on. Some proud parents smile smugly at their talented children, while troubled siblings whine that they are bored and want to go home.

As I sprint down the springy green track in the sunshine, on the last leg of the four by one hundred relay, and I see everyone from Salisbury A.C. screaming and cheering for me 'ELL-LIE! ELL-LIE!' I know there is nothing I would rather be doing. Without a doubt, Salisbury A.C. is what Salisbury means to me!

*Ellie Carlisle*

OLD SARUM FLYING CLUB is located in Salisbury near to the ruins of the Old Salisbury cathedral. It is a small club which has a canteen, where you can sit and have a drink between flying lessons.

A flying lesson will show you the whole of Salisbury. It can take you over the old cathedral, and you would see the main sights of Salisbury and the surrounding area. If you wanted to you could even fly around your house and see your village or town.

I went for my first flying lesson on my birthday. As soon as we took off I was allowed by my instructor to fly the plane myself.

We flew over the ruins of the old cathedral, over the whole of Salisbury and over Downton to see my house. Then we flew over other areas like Romsey and Fordingbridge. We even flew over Australia! Actually, Australia is a really big carving in the chalk on the side of a hill. It's just the outline of the country with the name written beneath it. A half an hour trial lesson would cost about £40, and an hour's lesson would cost about £80! Old Sarum is a very nice area with plenty of fields and hills.

The club has a wide range of planes, which include one-seater to four-seater light aircraft, micro-lights and gliders. Old Sarum Flying Club holds about twenty planes.

The views when you're in a plane are amazing. You can see for miles around, and everything below you looks really small. You normally fly at around 2,000 metres up and at about 100 miles per hour.

I think that Old Sarum is the nicest place in Salisbury I've ever seen, and I hope in future years that people will enjoy it as much as I have.

*Amanda Perry*

I STARTED WITH STAGE 65' youth theatre about two years ago when I first came from Germany to live in England. I enjoyed meeting all the other people, but didn't think that acting was really my thing. I was still enjoying it and didn't want to leave the theatre, so I thought that the technical side and back-stage assistance would be a lot more interesting. The first performance I helped with was 'Into the Woods' which was very successful. I wasn't sure what I was going to do, so I helped with stage design, which included painting, sewing, screwing things together, saw-ing, etc. As there were quite a lot of us backstage, I was asked whether I would like to do the follow-spotting during the performance. I agreed, and was shown what to do with the follow-spot up in the lighting box. It was great fun and very interesting seeing everyone down on stage in their fairy-tale costumes. It was fantastic.

After this play I thought I'd give acting a go, and did a production called 'Titan's Claw', which was about the sinking of the Titanic in 1912. This was fun, but the acting part didn't appeal to me very much as it made me feel very nervous and insecure. Salisbury Youth Theatre has put on some great plays in the past and it is so much fun being a part of the company and sharing that feeling without being one of the actors.

I love making clothes, so for the next performance, 'Animal Farm' (which is about animals taking over and becoming just like humans), I thought it would be fun making and creating different animal costumes. Being part of the backstage crew is just as important as being an actor. I think people often forget that without the costume assistance, lighting, stage management and backstage crew, nothing would work.

You have to commit yourself just as much as the actors to rehearsals. There is a lot of pressure to get costumes finished, as three months is not a long time to get all the mea-surements and costumes ready for about forty people. It is very interesting and great fun doing research on how animals walk and look, sewing, stitching, sticking, dyeing and dirtying down costumes to make them look like farm animals. The best bit is when they are all finished and seeing what you have achieved.

During the performances wardrobe assistance is very important, especially when sheep lose their fur, hens their beaks, and pigs can't get their ears on, in which case wardrobe has to stand by and help come up with a solution to these problems.

*Robynne Hammer*

# So where is our favourite place to relax or find adventure?

AS I SAT DOWN AT THE TABLE, recently occupied, and looking so, I looked around me at the busy scene before my eyes. A mother of two strolled past me, quickly raising her tray as one of the following children rushed ahead of her to get to an empty seat. There were at least seven queuers to the right of me, which almost stretched to the halfway point marked by two pillars on either side of the room. I glanced up to the long counter behind which many staff were bustling about, collecting hamburgers or drinks from the array of machinery and hot plates. My gaze crept upwards and rested on the square panels that displayed the menu, amongst other things, such as pictures or value meals. I also noticed the red and yellow emblem of McDonald's.

As I waited patiently for the vegetarian meal I had ordered, I looked behind me to see if Mindy, whom I was meeting here, was coming. I watched disappointedly as a young mother wrestled with the door whilst trying to get her pushchair inside. A gust of wind outside rattled the littered drink cans and blew the rubbish up the street slightly.

A lady carefully swept her hair back into place before hurrying across the road.

A smartly dressed man was talking into a mobile phone whilst dodging a mother shouting at her son to stop messing about in the road as well as holding tightly to his little sister.

I sighed and turned back to the activity in the restaurant. I glanced at my watch and shifted my feet as a mop was hastily pushed under the table, swept about a bit and withdrawn. The cleaner swiftly moved on to the next table without a word. The young mother with the pushchair had almost got to the front of the queue. I turned to face the door again and smiled and waved as Mindy came in.

*Catherine Mawdsley*

*Friends Laura Boyd*

Jhonathan

Shaun

peaple

me

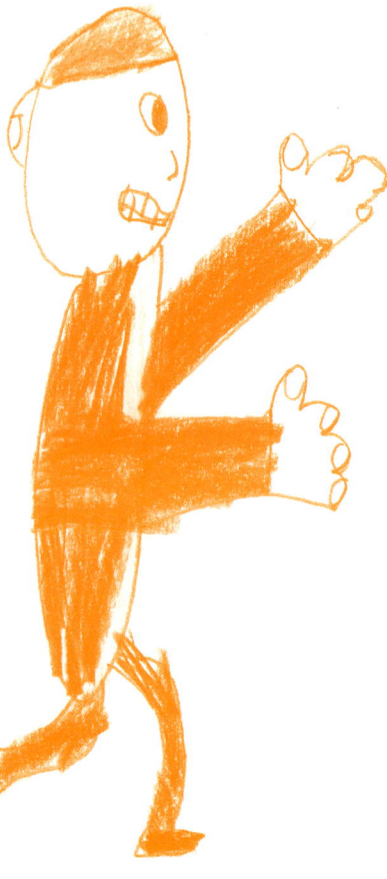

Play Field *David*

I WENT TO WILTON HOUSE LAST SATURDAY. There are lots of slides and a gigantic house. The Earl of Pembroke lives in it. There is a whispering seat. I think that the best thing in Wilton House is the rope you go from one side to the other. I usually meet my friends there. There are bridges going over some small rivers with fish in. There are some really big slides. One of them is a tunnel. If you go down on your jumper you go fling out of the other end!

*Timothy Oliver*

MY FAVOURITE PLACE in Salisbury is Elizabeth Gardens. I like the name and the park. In the park my favourite apparatus is the roundabout because it goes VERY FAST! There are lots of flowers. I like the tulips best - the red ones. Sometimes there's an ice cream, mmmm! We paddle in the stream, we play in the park, we feed the ducks and we walk in the gardens.

*Elizabeth Lawson*

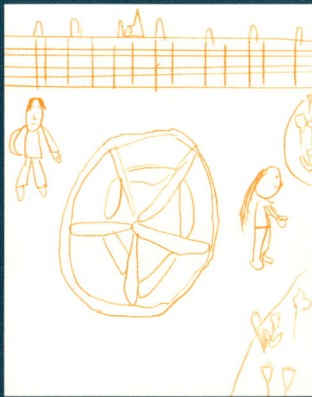

Elizabeth Gardens
*Elizabeth Lawson*

MY FAVOURITE PLACE is The Old Castle. Because it has lovely Desserts and very, very, very nice Dinners. My mum and my mum's boyfriend take me, my brother and sister come too. Sometimes our Nan takes us. And sometimes we take our Nan. I usually have pasta there and I always have a Knicker-blocker-glory *(sic)*, and I always eat it all. There is a very steep slide. There is a den that I discovered. Whenever we go to The Old Castle and we have to go home I always hide.

*Ashley Pennell*

WILTON HOUSE IS A PLAY PARK BUT BIG. It has four big slides and one tube slide. It has a places for 5 and unders with a slide, swings and a trampoline.

There is a big trampoline by the tube slide and two big slides. There are swing boats and monkey bars, picnic tables, nature walks and big gardens. There is a big river, big open spaces and lots of wild flowers.

Wilton is right next to Salisbury, and if you are coming from Salisbury, quite near to the front of Wilton. Wilton House is owned by a very rich family who have opened it to the public. They have a gift shop and car park. You can buy a season ticket, otherwise you have to pay each time you go in. There is a place to buy food and drink and a place to buy ice lollies.

I like Wilton House.

*Peter Robinson*

Salisbury Swimming Pool *Sophia Sample*

MY FAVOURITE PLACE in Salisbury is the swimming pool.
Because I like it when I go down the big slide. I like it when I go
under the water because I like scaring my brother. I even like
going down to the bottom - then I can push my brother under
the water too.

*Tracy Hogan*

Swimming things
*Natasha Long*

# ALL THE BEST
# FOR SALISBURY'S
# FUTURE

........................

I HAVEN'T LIVED IN SALISBURY all of my life. I moved here two and a half years ago, and think it is a great place to 'hang out' with your friends. Most of the schools are situated in the town and it is really fun to be able to go into town after school. Salisbury is a great place to live in 1999.

*Kerri Chalk*

THE CATHEDRAL VERY
  BEAUTIFUL,
   but also very old.
    The museums are great,
    plus artefacts of every date.
  I love to live in Salisbury.
  Cycle on flat land, play out
   with all your mates, I love
     to live in Salisbury
       because it is so great.
   Clown About to play,
     tanks and army camps,
       Salisbury Plain, Clinton
         Cards. I love to live
in Salisbury.

*David Livesey*

Exhibit in the
Military Museum
*Arthur Webb*

LAST YEAR ON THE 2ND OF JULY A VERY SPECIAL PERSON
came into my life, my little
brother Ty.

I was thrilled with the arrival of
this baby, as were many other
people in my family, and he
could not have been born in a
better place. There are trees to
climb, five rivers that over the
years I'm sure he'll fall into,
parks and fields to play in, wild
animals such as foxes and
badgers, moles and squirrels
to marvel at.

When he is older I'm sure he
will enjoy learning the history
of Salisbury from Old Sarum
and Stonehenge to the by-pass
rows of today. I hope he grows
up in a warm, natural, good
community, where the treasures
of days gone past shine in the modern world of today.

*Grace Naug*

Jousting at Old Sarum *Charley Lagler Duff*

## *So, for Salisbury and its district, as we move into the new millennium there is good and bad, pride in past achievements, and hopes for a bright future.*

ROLLING HILLS GIVE BIRTH TO
THE FIVE RIVERS,
Which like fingers, all converge at the palm.
Salisbury is this palm.
The snake-like tributaries slither down,
Meeting no other, and only stop at
Their final resting place.

At this resting place the flowers bed down,
Forming a bright duvet on the ground,
Covering the mud.
Shrubs and bushes grow their coloured berries,
And the trees put on their green overcoats,
Reaching to the sky.

Old Sarum, the ruins upon the hill,
Show a lot about the historic
South of Wiltshire.
And the medieval part of Salisbury
Is full of old world history,
Wherever we look.

Salisbury Cathedral towers high above,
The statues and gargoyles staring down
Over the city,
And the fourteenth-century buildings,
With wattle and daub walls and black beams
Where our ancestors lived.

But most of all, Salisbury now is a place
Where everyone goes to meet people
And have some fun.
It is as busy as any town,
With thousands of shoppers making their way,
Through the crowded streets.

*Anthony Munro*

TODAY (22ND FEB. 1999) IS MY BIRTHDAY, and I was born here in Salisbury 86 years ago, and apart from the 1939-45 war years, and a few times away, due to my work, I have spent and lived all these years here, and never had a wish to move away.

As I was growing up, so was Salisbury. I well remember walks to Laverstock Downs, Harnham Downs, top of the old chalk pit and along to the Race Plain, or go across the Broken Bridges site, and back via Lower Bemerton and Churchfields. Another walk was along the Bishopdown Path to Old Sarum, around the two outer rings, etc, and then back via Stratford and Butts Fields.

All these districts form part of Salisbury with its extra housing, schools, transport, water and electrical services, etc., all blending in with older parts of the town, restored buildings, Victoria Park, Green Croft, Riverside Walk, and not forgetting the Cathedral and its fine Close. More recently we have the old St Edmunds Church made into a fine Arts Centre, a City Hall, new Playhouse, Leisure Centre, play areas, sports, and its many events, not forgetting a new hospital, many retirement homes, and the Churchill and Elizabeth Gardens.

We shall soon reach to year 2000, and I am sure Salisbury and District will meet it with much pride at what has been achieved during the last century.

It was due to a great amount of planning work, meetings, etc, over the years, and will do the same in the coming years.

All the best for Salisbury's future. Thank you.

*Mr M.C. Patience*

St Francis's Church
*Sarah Kirkpatrick*

Duck feeding *Hayley Harding*

The Close *Jonathan Scammell*

S is for spire, tall and proud.

A is for Avon that runs through the town.

L is for leisure centre where we keep fit.

I is for illumination, the cathedral is lit.

S is for Stonehenge, an ancient place.

B is for buildings, so full of grace.

U is for understanding people, who if there
was an accident would take pity.

R is for rivers that run through the city.

Y is for youth clubs, where you can have fun
and make new friends.

*Rebecca Allender*

High Street Gate *Lauren May Campbell*

SALISBURY IS A HISTORIC TOWN, and you become used to always seeing all of the historical sites and buildings. But when you stop and really think about how old they are, and really look at them, it is quite amazing and it gives you a shiver down your spine.

*Katie Allen*

# INDEX OF PLACES AND SUBJECTS

# INDEX OF PLACES AND SUBJECTS
*continued*